These poems employ powerful and often original use of language to embody perceptions of a reality both personal and objective in their immediacy.

I honestly think you will enjoy the humour nestled therein without losing the primary messages altogether. Many of the poems are indeed compelling, exhibiting both challenging complexity and underlying simplicity. I therefore think the collection is worth a good investment of your time with every verse deserving a close and attentive reading.

Geoffrey Jackson, Retired Teacher of Literature.

Phase of a Monster and Wild Roses

Cadence & Lyrics

OLUREMI FAYE-ADEMOLA

Copyright © 2024 Oluremi Faye-Ademola.

All rights reserved. No part of this book may be reproduced, stored, or transmitted by any means—whether auditory, graphic, mechanical, or electronic—without written permission of both publisher and author, except in the case of brief excerpts used in critical articles and reviews. Unauthorized reproduction of any part of this work is illegal and is punishable by law.

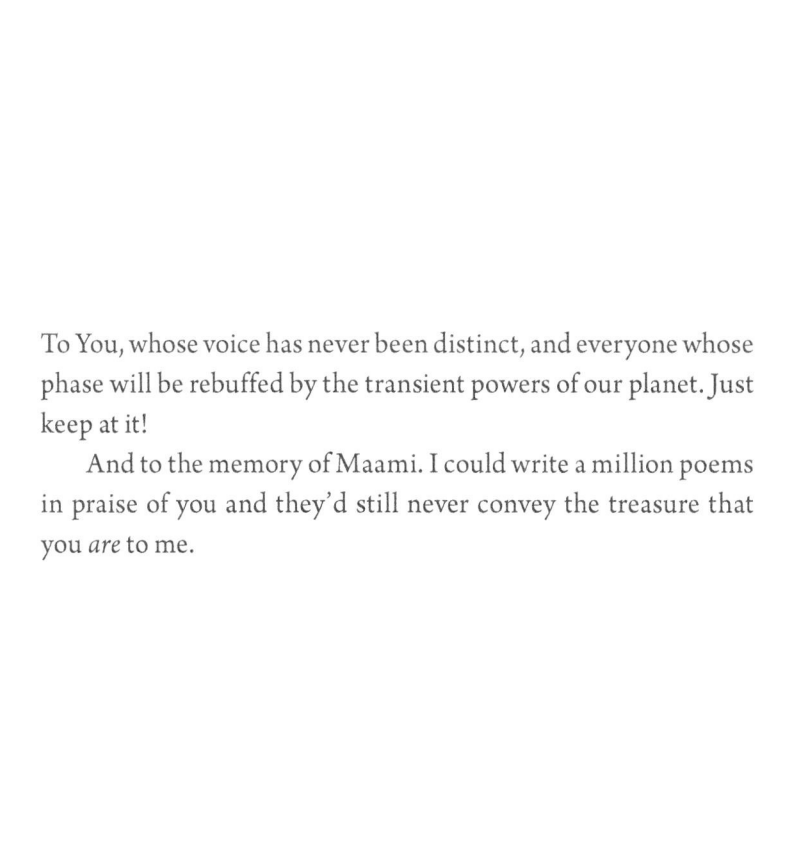

To You, whose voice has never been distinct, and everyone whose phase will be rebuffed by the transient powers of our planet. Just keep at it!

And to the memory of Maami. I could write a million poems in praise of you and they'd still never convey the treasure that you *are* to me.

Contents

Preface ix
Acknowledgements xi
Introduction xiii

Shadows and Silhouettes 1
My Great Grandmother's Garden 4
Coffee Clauses 7
Job Riddles 8
Madness on the Municipal 11
Remnants 15
Cluttered 18
Purple Grief 20
Sonnet (Agony of Peace) 22
Wasted Investiture 23
Little Yellow Pill 25
The Canine and the Feline 27
Gift of Controversy 30
April 14th, 2022 34
Cheeseball 35
A Dance of Freedom 37
Gracefully I Wear Me 40
Colour Charades 42
I Dare to Question Death 45

By the Willow Trees	48
In the Still…	50
Cloud Respite	51
Les Faux Amis	53
Everything has Ears	56
Let the Poet Live	58
You Befuddle Me, Truth	60
Stitch in the Eardrums	62
What is … the Night?	64
Dear Ol' Jim	65
College Shenanigans	68
Stellar Rush	71
Epitaph	73
Elegy	73
Words in any Language	75
Estrangement	77
The Right Ones	79
Hadassah	81
An African Child	84
Between the Poet and the Songster	88
Upon the Midnight Hours	89
The World's too much of a Judge	92
Entreaties of the Pragmatist	95
The Frame	97
Postboxes	98
Spring Angels	99
When you said Goodbye	101
Distractions at the Square	103
Written in August	106
Eyes of Innocence	108
Psalm 419	109

Preface

(How it all began)

My earliest recollection of poetry performance was at a now defunct event called 'Zeta Kappa Phi' (ZKP) at the Obafemi Awolowo University, Ile-Ife, Osun State, Nigeria. I must have been about 9 or 10 years old at the elementary school then. Although events at that period now remain somehow sketchy, I recall that I attended an audition at the school hall where I made substantive impression on the panel of judges, as I will never forget the resounding applause that followed after speaking my lines.

My next encounter with stage poetry would be at the Efunyela hall on the occasion of late Chief Obafemi Awolowo's 70th birthday. In all modesty, I would not affirm that I felt much more sensation as I had felt previously at the ZKP event. However, in retrospect, maybe there wasn't anything particularly special, but I will never forget that 'my lines' were confident and articulate enough to laud the late statesman's political ambition so that this time, I did not just receive an applause, I received standing ovation across the grand banquet hall. Both of these separate occurrences have always stood out for me, over time amongst others whenever I endeavour to trace the origin of my penchant for poetry.

Acknowledgements

I would like to thank everyone who has contributed in one way or the other directly and indirectly to the production of this book.

To God Almighty my Redeemer, Comforter and Sustainer in the eye of every storm.

To the legacies of my parents of blessed memory, I always wanted to do something in your honour and names. Thank you more than a million, Maami, for your diligence and selflessness and my Papa too.

To my sisters, Dr Adetola Olasoji (JP) and Hon. Justice Omolara Adejumo respectively, you both held up my hands where I should have sunk. I owe so much to you, thank you immensely.

My late sister, Monisola Omolola (I dedicated 'Written in August' to your memory) you had so much to live for, but heaven gained you over in your prime. You are always fondly remembered.

I would like to thank my husband, Segun. You have given me room to explore. You are also a ready and useful resource when struggling with translating some of my indigenous themes.

To Angela Phelan and Geoffrey Jackson (fellow poets at Putney Verse Workshop), I am very much indebted to you both. I ran to you, Angela for proofreading/editing and you obliged me nobly in spite of your busy schedule.

To all my students of poetry (both old and current) I am grateful that this is not relegated to just a guilty pleasure on my part, it feels heavenly when we dive into the poems and I am always inclined to refine the craft of poetry appreciation and writing. You all inspire me greatly.

My heart is full of thanks to both late Dr Tai Solarin and Madam Sheila Solarin (founders of Mayflower School, Ikenne). Your institution of learning bequeathed to me and several others such academic excellence to take on the world!

And finally, to the AuthorHelp team, especially Robin, I came by freighted with much doubts and anxieties, but you allayed all of the fears by your patience, professionalism and transparency. Thank you, a great deal.

Introduction

When the monster calls, no one shows readiness to let it into their space. Because it is presumably formidable, hideous and terrifying, it forces entry, then it becomes enormously arduous to manage its menace. In 'Phase of a Monster and Wild Roses,' many situations present like monsters. Upsetting childhood experiences, Mental frailty, Grief, Estrangements, Rebellion, Nostalgia and Fatal errors are some subject-matters surveyed.

There is a further zooming on issues bordering on individual strength of character, integrity and self-esteem in the wake of social media infiltration. False concepts about others, Mistrust, Exploration of life and death, Self-consciousness and assertion, Futility and Vanity make some thematic issues as well. Whereas some of the poems in the collection are intentioned comics E.g. 'Colour Charades' and 'College Shenanigans,' other sterner themes are intended to readdress readers' views and outlook on life in general. 'Gift of Controversy' is one example.

In addition, some poems are a turning point of Reawakening, Healing, Renewed Hope and Optimism. E.g. 'Remnants' and 'Cluttered.' After the monster phase (face) of fear, stagnation and the vicissitude of the seasons, wild roses appear with beauty and thorns. The travails never completely vanish, but at most the ugliness dissipates. Anyone who endeavours to harvest wild roses with a diligent mind may heal swifter from the monster's ugliness and distress.

In conclusion, readers are cautioned to be prepared for an ambivalent adventure as the poems will certainly take them on a journey. A journey of battles fought and won, those matters springing forth from unpopular cadre, of false friendships and intent, of the brevity of life, of building resilience in the face of obstacles, of man's quests that can hardly be sated, of loss, purpose and identity, ***where a man fills his entire time with enormous deeds, then loses his being in the business of his acts.***

I wish you all the muse!

Shadows and Silhouettes

Shadows and Silhouettes
They tell a common tale
About the interface
Of Dark and Light

Shadows,
Long and dark
Must come with rays

Long before caravans, pyramids,
Radars in lofty ships
Are shadows to man.

In Eden or in Heaven
Dark becomes a renegade.
He mutinies.
****
Without contrition,
none whatsoever…

War is activated.

Then the chute!

Dark
He takes some Light along
So Shadows, long and dark

Are a rebound
When Light is glee.

Silhouettes
They are just so like Shadows
In every form and frame
These are not born though,
By chaos in some remote planets
They are an ingenuity of man

Silhouettes are dark too.
They trend only
With a measure of light
They are 2D.
Like Shadows,
Without a depth.
They are gothic
In every sense of art.

The King of them are Stars
They need Dark too
If they must gleam and glitter.

So Dark is a common ally

There
Is
Some
Light
In
Dark

Without
A
Shadow
Of
Doubt.

PHASE OF A MONSTER AND WILD ROSES

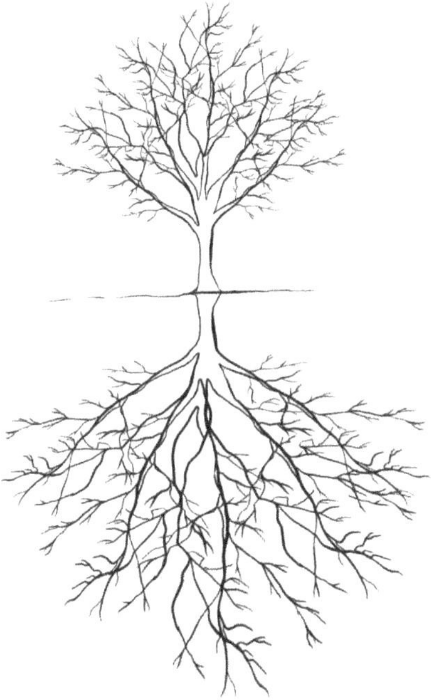

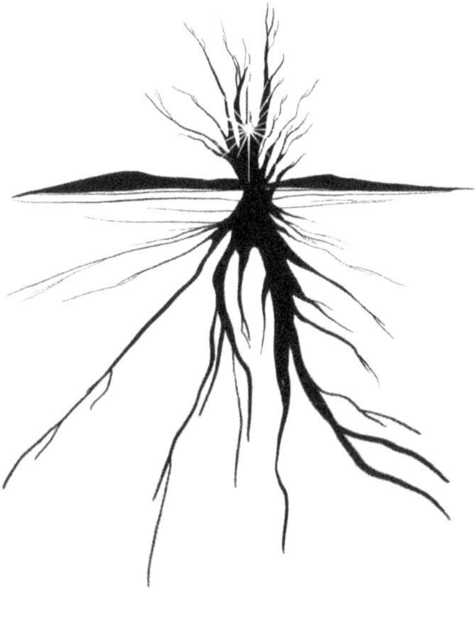

My Great Grandmother's Garden

The yard's fairly broad
As far as I recall
Cross-breeds
Peculiar plots
Exotic species
Native climbers
Hybrid of vegetables
Miscellany of herbs

Sugarcane stalks.

In my great grandmother's rear garden,
There's even cotton
Embedded within a copse

So, when we fall
And bruise the knees
Great granny, she pulls it fresh
From her fenced bed
Wipes the clot with care
Then cooks bitterleaf soup
To savour with cocoyam boluses
A fit of the sulks at first,
Often, then ends in ecstasy.

Sugar rush
It always starts the race, the chase.
Bang!!!
And there … we're flat.

Four dozen and two,
Still,
On the countertop,
On a porcelain tray,
Are twigs of bitterleaves
Spread out.
Ready to be sweetened
By the magic of a wring
Just the way the leaves were wrung
In my great grandmother's scullery.

Cane sugar.

The fiend from which to flee.

*Bitterleaves are a type of plant used in cooking, and native to the African tropics. Of late, it's been reputed to possess high medicinal benefits, and used to treat many ailments.

Coffee Clauses

Last winter, we had coffee in Corsica
With a crony thought to be well-known
'Twas an oddly moment indeed
Ugly mugs on dainty saucers
Two teaspoons of noun phrases
One and half cubes of adverbials
Coffee mate of modal verbs
And a splash of adjectives
A steaming pot of coffee clauses
That served to scald our velum
She beckoned the patisserie, of course
Crusted croissants of conjunctions
Toasted raisins of sticky apostrophes
'Tis a teaser to the brain
And a puzzle to the mind
When you meet a **pedagogue.**

Job Riddles

Choosing a career path sometimes feels animated
A tricky casino, like the game of gambling

You may never stop to observe details
Or tell riddles therein with passage of time

Some jobs dictate your base
They chart your course, your destination.

Other jobs are petulant – like spoilt brats
They incessantly seek your attention

There are jobs with self – will and haughtiness
You must let them take the lead

Many jobs are cool but lackluster
Just 9 to 5

Some jobs will plan the menu, dominate the kitchen
Then set the dinner table.

Other jobs daze and spin you round
Globetrotting, severely jetlagged

Many jobs erode you of self-esteem
So, keep back your damn ego at home

There are jobs replete with complexities
You disguise every time, mapping out new strategies

Some jobs only need your muscles
Come with brains and fall out with the foreman.

Other jobs are very frail, blunders are impending
Leaving you with lifetime scandals

Many jobs are noble, they're like a cause
You cannot simply flout the call – No way!

There are jobs with vast creativity
A test of your profundity and novelty, they are

Some jobs are deprival, draining you of vigour
They overcompensate with fringe benefits

Other jobs are vile, dreadful jobs
They scream shady, illicit and depravity

Many jobs operate colonies
They have defied the odds of irrelevance

There are jobs that are grossly vain
They have no enduring purpose

Some jobs are extremely volatile, like benzol
If caught up, they burst into infernal flames

Other jobs are a trauma campsite, they sap of fervour
You may shed off an ocean of pathos

The moon, the sun and stars, held up in space
They do jobs of unfathomable dimension.
Leaving men enthralled.

And yet again, a few jobs are just so uncanny
A trade with outlandish speech signs,
symbols and mannerisms.

What riddles does your job ricochet?

Madness on the Municipal

Come my child, board the Municipal.
It is long and rugged
With some classic depression
And some helpless country wrecks
Yesterday, I ran into Willie
His shirts with stale sweat
Round the armpit, yet
With a smile of rectitude,
Revealed a couple of wasted dimples.

The trip may tarry
A weary to the soul
Never mind to shut your eyes
When they do feel a fatigue
Or should you feel a slumber
And mind the gaps
When it is time to dribble
Constables give hot stinking slaps
They think it's shameless hangovers
And carry all weight of frustration
The masses ought to share.

One more thing,
Did you gauge your alarm?
That's an awful little prompt
And a device to let you know
When the driver pulls up
And the Municipal is at the garage.

Oh child, you meet some aliens
Fierce, eccentric, weird aboard
Sometimes apparelled bizarrely
Only to evade the fare.
They look scary and gaunt
Their hair stands in locks
And those with merchandise
Flinging them in eager faces.
Reign of the charlatans
Broad daylight wrapped up
In the depth of dense ignorance

If a scuffle ensues
I pray you child, hold your peace
For you are an infant
You will not comprehend
A schoolboy
With all the juvenile innocence
Do not cogitate on these
Lest you be discomfited
They are a city bus scenario.

Learn your hard sums – Algebra, Geometry
Calculus and Probability
Every bit of nonsensical arith – matrix
And your parts of speech
Lexis and structure
They make you sound dead posh
I used to like the complete metamorphosis
Of the Anopheles muss…qui…toe
You may visit the science lab

Not too long from now
Pay great attention to your titration
My child, I beg of you – this is important

Grandma once gave to me
A tumbler of steamed herbs
To cure some stubborn fever
It remains a mystery
I did not have any clues
Of the chemical condiments
Even when it made me
All the more feverish
She said that knocks down a bit
Before it makes well again
Like QUININES
It is indeed a mystery

The Municipal is another mystery
A witty journey of life
It terminates, sometimes fatally
Oftentimes, I'd wished I never had to board
In a bid to avoid those desperate folks
But more dreadful eyes
With more fretful cares
Crawl the roads in strands
They would not board the Municipal

It is a different world in here
My child, yet it teaches a lesson
A lesson of a lifetime.
But we shall alight
From this scene of insanity

Hoping to gracefully arrive at the bend
That leads us right to the mission
Number 12
Right there, we will remember to say
The 121 chapter of the Psalms.

Oh child, it is a little life
But of massive madness
And tons of mystery
Thitherto we shall stay resolute
As we boldly look up
To the floods of heaven
To quench our insatiable souls.

Remnants

(Late 70s, a fairly decorated large sitting room, a strikingly beautiful middle-aged lady and a child of about 5-7 years old sobbing and kicking in the typical mannerism of a child. In the most affectionate manner, the woman begins reciting what seemed to sound like a mantra in an indigenous dialect to the child. Gradually, the child's gasps subdues and the ambience regains some tranquillity. These chants are what have been referred to as 'Oriki')

THAT,
was the voice of the queen of my life.
And THOSE,
were the adulations
in which I was consistently drowned
growing up.
It's crystal clear
these sonorous chants are a symphony
a masterpiece of a thousand pedigree
that may never be flawed.

Nobody really schooled me about self-respect.
even though I was always groomed
to respect everyone else around me
regardless of who they were.
Not in any strict order of hierarchy,
but just a few of those
whom I had to respect.
I had to respect my parents,
had to revere my grandparents.
At school, I had to show deference to teachers.
Teachers were mini-gods

when the cosmos claimed
it was inclined to innocence.
And what?
With those bully-about seniors,
they, too, must be shown some regards.
Besides, I took that Benjamin slot
within my household.
So I had a long string of siblings
to whom I was duty bound
to smudge heavily with some respect.
By the time it was 360 degrees full circle,
Respect had been pizza arced
And none was left to give myself.
As even an older, naughty neighbour alike,
Squirted on me some disesteem.

In my ignorance,
I should believe all recipients
took their stake, and did fair with it.
How wrong I was!
And was I found not to be respectful,
some sour, long-winding saga.
Does these resonate?
Bruises, battery and broken blisters?
Talk of trajectories, not laid out
with smooth skinned velvet and voile.

Now Earth has sucked spans of rainfall
Finally, …
I rekindle what seems to have lapsed
Knowing just as many wrongs
May never have been intended

They may be oversights -
Or some domiciliary sloppiness

I resuscitate what's left
Of a thing of prestige, pristine in its form.
I shuffle and juggle it around.
Pity though, I still don't quite get it
as intoned like 'maami' used to sink me in them
yet, I take the remnants,
travel back in time
and like dripping diamonds,
I relish myself in those moments
of impeccable splendour.

Glossary

Maami literally translates to 'my mother'
Oriki praise poetry or mantra chants are a verbal art. It is peculiar to individual dynasties of cultural landscapes and heritage in Nigeria.

Cluttered

3:45am, the haze is incredible
Like the forecast forewarned.
A nimble spectre swooshes
Into the denseness of many rooms.

What are these nothingness of mass?
It's nearly dawn, yet it feels a twilight.
Some invincible dogged might
Having neither substance nor stability.

At another shackland, foggier yet.
Scraps, squashed sheets, shrunken sheaths
Strewn around like an old shrew's chamber
With a drab hope of clarity.

Time checked, 4:15am.
Further into clouds of vagueness,
Drifts of haze and smoke invade
The entire landscape. Fells are buried.

To the fore, still in the smog,
Comes the sudden wrench…
Familiar creaks, flicks, crackles,
Shrill effects, knock-offs,
Strident pulls, etcetera, etcetera.

Portrait of the past, fuzzy frames
Fall off the grimy walls. All standing
In disarray, frail and fragile.
The fray, a thing foreshadowed.

Head goes giddy – like fireworks
It's 5am on the watch. Chirrrp! chirrrp!
They seem to sing in tune
Celebrating fragments of a thousand fracas.

Daybreak.

The smog dissipates.
Floras greener, fountains flowing
The bulrush stands hearty.

A light head,
A Tabula Rasa
Set to spring anew.

Purple Grief

Because you left on that October noon,
And you did not duel with Agony,
But you took charge of your passing
Like an empress would her empire
I will not compose 'the blues'

You were the mother eagle with great tenacity
Your soul mated with pedagogy, propriety, ethics
And nothing ever in the similitude of a mercenary
Your spirit stood strikingly at variance with avarice
You taught me that beneath all of the world's
Gloss and glamour lie a delicate veneer of vanity.

You loved the Lord and would be taciturn
At sunrise until Quiet time is diligently observed
How you came to be voracious of the bible!
That I watched you in the cock-crow cry
A call to worship, a clarion to rescue
From the paths of peril and from worldliness.

I listened as you would make supplications
On behalf of your children, the family,
The church, the clerics and your land
You made inventory of the slightest petition
And steadfast in the ideal, you were.
Barely shifting your focus.

Once, it was customary to hire wailers
In a bid to magnify the extremeness of a dirge
But I have cautiously reviewed the art of grief
And I am thrust into clarity
Of the wholeness in your exit.

Now I sit in this oasis
thanks to your handsome bequests,
On my right hand are an armoury of God's word
And on the left are a treasury of insights
For all of these and more, I am eternally grateful.

So, rest on mother
In the hearth and abode of your Maker.

Sonnet (Agony of Peace)

Where my wounds are inflicted, I'd choose
In haste, I'd lay my skin for every blow
A defiant scathe, proof of a heart's bruise
Why won't with time they scar then glow?
Behold the repugnant laceration
To heal, to be whole defy
Only I live with gory sensation
Of blasts cutting deep by the by

Still, I'll strive binding my soul and mind afar
Aye, the hurts conceal some trophies won
I have learned to trust without an eye ajar
The way of pardon, and peace now reborn
So great in strength when all the fractures mend
And full of mirth which all the raptures send

Wasted Investiture

The brine in my lids
Is short for insolvency
Beneath the yoke of the black knight
My breast is left dehydrated
I weep, yet pardon I must 5
This unatoned trespass
Shoved aside like some misdemeanour.

Or else,
It grooms wide into a yellow bile
My gall bladder should burst 10
And splatter it through
The stench pollutes my gut
My palate poisoned with the sour dose

We had sprung from the same soil
We had palled up. I mean 15
I palled around in ignorance
Thought we had a history.

But friendship untried, untested, unproven
Is totally ephemeral
Like fashion 20
Impressive for a season … fizzling effortlessly

I must the demise of this enterprise now mourn
Which bore a seedling… then
Shrank
And plasmolysed.

But with due diligence I did irrigate
Or perhaps, inundated with bloated affection

It grew turbid and lost *'essence'*.

Little Yellow Pill

Little yellow pill
I loathe the look of you.
I detest the sight of you

You grate my guts
And twirl my throat
To soothe my bouts of pain.

Posing on the table
Waiting for my paunch
You make me well, they say.

You're not my choice
You're not my taste
You dreary yellow pill.

I am become your captive
I am become your slave
I writhe and rue upon a miss
Oh lurid yellow tab

Why not you change your colour?
Your shape?
At most, your size?

Perhaps a shade of green
And a size like Granny Smith.

The Canine and the Feline

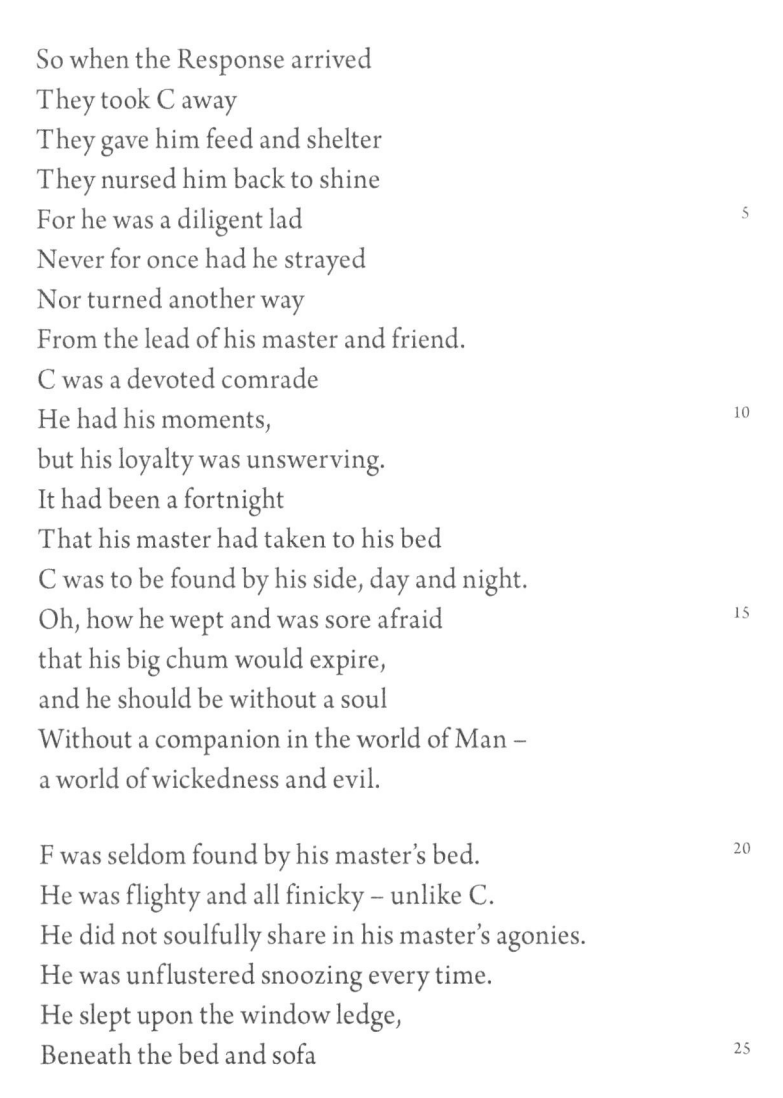

So when the Response arrived
They took C away
They gave him feed and shelter
They nursed him back to shine
For he was a diligent lad
Never for once had he strayed
Nor turned another way
From the lead of his master and friend.
C was a devoted comrade
He had his moments,
but his loyalty was unswerving.
It had been a fortnight
That his master had taken to his bed
C was to be found by his side, day and night.
Oh, how he wept and was sore afraid
that his big chum would expire,
and he should be without a soul
Without a companion in the world of Man –
a world of wickedness and evil.

F was seldom found by his master's bed.
He was flighty and all finicky – unlike C.
He did not soulfully share in his master's agonies.
He was unflustered snoozing every time.
He slept upon the window ledge,
Beneath the bed and sofa

Most often, by the floor of the hearth.
He dug his paws in the litter and turned it over
What a mess he made!
Yes, he cried, but his wail was not one of synchronization,
Only of hunger and thirst.
His master may have left a louvre loose upon the shutters...

Back in his new domicile,
C was living a day at a time.
And how he grieved for his master and friend.
For he was indeed sore stricken
More than a faithful shadow of his master
On the day of the funeral,
C was drenched in his tears.
The last to leave the mound.
Poor C won't shake this off so soon
And unready for rehousing.
The Response are holding up his ladder.

Well, well, well
Someone had said they caught sight of F the other day
Bragging on his breed
"I am an offspring of the Panthera and Felidae, roared he."
Now savage and roughly furred.
"If my master feeds and pampers me,
only then may I cast aside my pride.
"I beg to differ from C
who must have company by all means."
"I now hunt alone in the wild."
And with that he vaulted over to the other side.

This is the sorry business of the Feline and the Canine.
If somewhat, the universe be an adjudicator over the matter.   55

(This poem is partly inspired by a film I saw years ago. I have overtly used it to explore the subject of loyalty.)

Gift of Controversy

As twilight envelops the sun,
Behind the clouds, the moon sways
The skies overcast; firmaments wind down.

Again, dusk transfigures into dawn,
heralding sunrise.
A new day begotten, the world –
Wakeful to novel chances
Men, hopeful, their frets declare
Amidst pregnant turns and twists
Behold another gift of life!

How so easily we forget
That a gift is given for timeless withholding
But a loan is for a fleeting custody
To think that a gift will not strictly underscore liability
But a loan most resolute will render accounts
It is often so that we pay little or no details to our gifts
Which we may, by choice, cast aside with time
But duty imposes on us tributes to our loans
We nonetheless, refuse to highlight our gifts
For obvious reasons – no reviews, no audits
But a loan will shudder us down to the marrow
If casually handled. It is pricey.
Repayments have led some to the giggle house

We have often watched combatants
Transferring gifts of sentiments
To their offspring through comrades-in-arms
Like historic monuments.
When the warfront becomes stiff,
Many combatants have handed down keepsakes
Through pedigrees like monarchical feuds

Our loans only get a crafty shift,
Written off after a complex trajectory.

Do you not get it still?
That life may not, after all be a gift
Given we shall be stripped off it
One day unbeknownst, impromptu
Defying every material collateral.
And woe betides him who has lived life as a gift,
Forgetting the day, the hour he will render reports
In the boardroom of expert pawnbrokers.

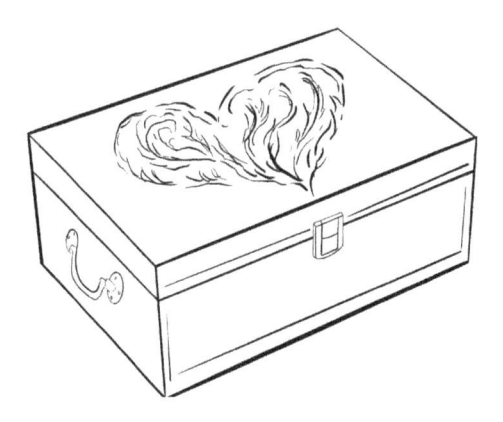

Do you ever hear of the book of life,
Or the day of reckoning?
No one keeps a ledger because he has given a gift.
A gift departs not to be reclaimed
Not to be reunited with the giver.
A loan travels on a precise mission
Within a time-stretch, returning accrued
Repossessed by the mortgagee should he default.

So, I fall into pensive mode
****
Life
Are you really,
truly,
exactly,
indisputably,
sincerely,
incontestably,
unquestionably,
assuredly,
honestly,
genuinely,
candidly,
precisely,
actually,
certainly,
irrefutably,
incontrovertibly,
unreservedly,
absolutely,
undeniably,

accurately,
undoubtedly,
definitely,
frankly,
unarguably,
affirmatively,
unequivocally,
clearly

a Gift?

April 14th, 2022

Another time of the year to embark on a quest within.
To be pensive, to speak volumes to me than to be spoken to
To pause the analogues, listening only to the rhythm of my heartbeat
To remind me of the NOW.

It's another time of the year to heal and to breathe anew
To utilize the verbs of perception in more adventurous ways
To create an octave of dissonance
Unravelled in rhymed sestet of assonance.

It's another time of the year
To not dignify anybody's queries by searching for desperate answers
To feel grateful for the beauty in the brokenness of life
To not simply burnish life in images.

To look to the future with nothing else, but hope renewed in Christ.

Cheeseball

The milk of human kindness
Everyone has had some.

No, I didn't, what colour is it?
Flax, amber or mellow yellow?

Don't be silly, it's just plain milk
Every one knows what it tastes like.

Ah well, does it taste farm fresh?
Like yogurt or condensed?

None of the above
Did you ever feed from the bottles?

And who was the milking cow?
Was yours curdy?

No, no, not until you make of it a milkshake
Then it goes frothy.
And turns berry, cream or blushing peach
With lactose, fructose and all.

Very well, are you the dairymaid?
Who comes to town at dawn?
The milk of human kindness
Everyone has had a measure.

Well then, if you must know
I was raised in the sanctuary.

And the milk of human kindness?
Did you manage to savour some?

Oh no, poor her, a teenage mum,
She left once I arrived.

Ah, ah, no wonder you are mean
She left with the mother's milk?

Sure, she did, and left me as well
A cheeseball.

A Dance of Freedom

The rostrum is all set
The wardrobe mistress
She lays out my costumes
Tonight, I dare the dance
It's the dance of freedom
A dance to fly or fall

The drummers are here
Apparelled in a loud brown
And a tinge of ivory 'ofi'
The Bata and the Konga
Across their shoulders, customarily.
Ayandele the lead drummer,
Suave and spiffy,
He smells of polished Iroko.
When he beats his Dundun
I must sway to the left
And sway to the right

But a clatter of Agogo
From a distance distracts me
I cannot decipher now
What the Gangan talks
Spectators encircle me
From furrowed fallen faces
My body rhythm, I can tell
Is out of tune

The move, undignified
My steps as well.
Out of alignment, I must have staggered.

Am I in a strange space?
Is this the land of ancestry?
My forebears, are they watching?
Are they squinting, peering intently?

I smell Shekere in the crowd
Someone sneaks it here
To steal 'oguro' from the tapper
But it rattles
Shekere stays distinct
From the palm wine gourd.

In a wave of frenzy,
I spin myself around
So that Ayandele calls for 'Saworo'
I still my body
Suddenly, the groove resumes
As the brass jingles…

I give the dance of a revolution.

Glossary

Bata a type of drum native to the Yoruba cultural dance
Gangan/Dundun 'talking drums'

Ofi a type of fabric delicately woven and traditionally worn on special occasions by the Yoruba ethnic group in Nigeria. It emanates from the old Oyo Empire.

Oguro a locally tapped unrefined wine from saps of certain palm trees.

Saworo 'brass bells'

Shekere a round shaped wide bottleneck musical instrument with loosely stringed beads or cowries tied round it.

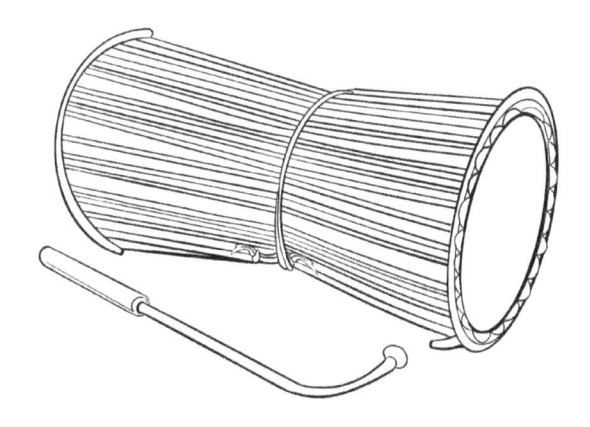

Gracefully I Wear Me

I squirm with dolour
A hollow so deep
To feel with much
And much, so much unreal
To polish the case
I keep the soul slack
The world revolving
Whirling me silly
A run without a goal
All in a bit to slay
Bondage for foolery
Dungeon of imbeciles
Look in my face
Tell me you do not capture the fatigue
No longer in the pride of youth,
I renounce the race,
the rush, the rat-tat-tat
A contest without a trophy
For who can conquer
The vastness of the deep
The immeasurable sensuality
of the universe
I have seen it all
Mere statement of arrogance
And the more fool me

So then,
I resolve to wisdom
To live again
Arise from the ashes of cynicism
I will wander afar off 30
From the alter ego
Wheeling me adrift
I will wear me alone
And wear me thence
with ultimate grace. 35

Colour Charades

(It's a game for two, or three at most.)

1st Player: What are the world's most favourite colours?
2nd Player: Ask Google.

1st Player: Google tells you colours of the rainbow, that's conventional.
2nd Player: Ask Alexa.

1st Player: Alexa is not cosmopolitan, S/he is rather unimpressionable.
2nd Player: Ask your teacher.

1st Player: My teacher's interests are geography and politics, not colours.
2nd Player: Ask your grandpa.

1st Player: My Grandpa will probably stay neutral; he's a relic, and that's dead boring.
2nd Player: Ask your grandma.

1st Player: Tut! my grandma is colour blind, that's sad, utterly!
2nd Player: Ask your uncle.

1st Player: My uncle has a red racing ride, and his fiancée's a redhead.
2nd Player: Ask your Dad.

1st Player: My Dad… he only wears black and white, now that's stereotypic.
2nd Player: Ask your Mum.

1st Player: My Mum, she thinks the world already of fruits and flowers. They're more evocative than colours.
2nd Player: Ha, ha, ha so ask your party freak aunt, then.

Aunt: (between listening to the charades and peeking at a Reader's Digest)
The world's best colours are:
Cockroach brown,
Mouse pink,
Chameleon cyan,
Monkey black,
Ghost white,
Lulu lavender and
Witchcraft wine

1st Player: (exclaiming)
Aunty, your choices are bizarre! None of them is on the spectrum! What a rainbow reverse!
Aunt: (with a tender smile)
Because, my pretty, there are no favourite colours of the world. The ideals of choicest colours are those burning bright like candles right in the dimness of the universe.

2nd Player: (with some solemnity)
Aphorism from the colour charades, FOR THE BRAVE ONES.

1st Player: I rest from weariness.

2nd Player: Aunty (looking askance at Aunt)
Aunty: Yes, my pretty.
2nd Player: Monsieur Lavender, who… who … er, who is HE?   40

(All remain as quiet as the churchyard)

I Dare to Question Death

Oh Death! who are you that you slay
From where do you come that you bray
You roam without a sisal upon your neck
You lurk in the corners, keeping a check
                      I dare to question you.

Oh Death! are you a retinue to any
That you may gather laurels so many
To parade in varying shades of colour
To whom do you owe this honour
                      I dare to question you.

Death! your appellations you do not fathom
The lips of men are like a restless phantom
Tell, I pray, how grotesque you are in visage
That you do not regard men of courage
                      I dare to question you.

Death! have you a domicile so vast
That you whisk away countless so fast
And I crave to know your benchmark
Are these folks who possess a hallmark
                      I dare to question you.

Oh Death, Death! do you not hold empathy
Why do you operate in gross apathy
To devour, to prey on mortals brusquely
Then watch their allies broken deeply
                      I dare to question you.

Ah Death! sit you might, and heftily
Who takes the sceptre from the lofty
And dare the heart of a warrior to feel
Is it bravery? Is it conquest? Or a meal
                        I dare to question you.   30

Oh Death! standing aloof, in spite of Mammon
And yourself seem a deity, foreign but common
You bow not in reverence to powers
Nor do you express desire for towers
                        I dare to question you.   35

Ah Death! terribly horrifying, solemnly
Hacking down is so not tasking – flippantly
Were you also present on the morn of creation
That you would not miss the apt soul location
                        I dare to question you.   40

Death! Death! why do you rhyme with birth
You clearly do not regard it at final breath
For the world rejoices upon the coming of a child
But you cast colossal grief upon a guild
                        I dare to question you.   45

Oh Death! are you so envious of day
That you covet it in altered way
Tell me are you solely a debit
And to whom do you repay the remit
                        I dare to question you.   50

Death! you repose in the tombs
While you skirt around the wombs
Are you not utterly ashamed
That you spark the soul aflame
                        I dare to question you.

But Death! you are a worthy leveller
The server of doom round a' dweller
Or so princes will charm with tiara and gaiety
And kings will enchant with purple of royalty

But none can demystify what placates you.

So, Death! be justice and be fair
Since you comprehend human despair
And death, an enigma of symmetry
Who rolls around as ultimate jury
                        Be justice and be fair!

By the Willow Trees

I love to write upon your face
When you are placid
And when you are tepid

When the ducklings glide not
And the cygnets are resting still
By the bank, about the reeds

When the frame of you
Is beaming by the first rays

I long to write bold, emphatic words
Unpunctuated, with minimal periods.

My words, a dazzling mirage
Upon your face and a centrepiece
Of your glistening flow

Though ripples may redesign the syllables
Through the gentle breeze
Your eye may ruffle

The winds may howl with gales
Ripping apart morphemes of my epigrams

And buoying up the eye rhymes of my limerick

Twill not quench the flames of my quest

OLUREMI FAYE-ADEMOLA

To re-edit, realign and rekindle
The purity of your lashes
And the texture of your brows

I will imprint therefore
Upon your face like a cuddy wifter
The symphony of my cantata

And the ecstasy of my sonnet
I will strive to see you never cringe again

Beneath the apathy of a make-up artisan
Upon the pages of your eye view.

In the Still...

In the muffled crackling of dry Leaves
In the casual caress of mighty Conifers
In the awesome dentition of Alligators
And the formidable jawline of Felines
In the aggression of turbulent Oceans
In the boom of Thunder, whizzes of Lightning
Whooshing and swooshing of Whirlwinds
In the cloudiest of Days, scorch of Sun
And in the temperament of tangled Thoughts...

****

I will be **STILL** and know YOU are God.

Cloud Respite

They say you're gone.
How?
Gone and laid to rest.
With no compassion
They did shove you
Into space, I guess
Although their claim is
You fizzled out with the clouds
Fists in gloves of velvet
These ones wear
In anguish, I inquired
Did they mark the spot?
A nebulous affair, they rant

My chest grinding and ripping
I am numb.
My head, BLANKS OUT!
I feel so very forlorn
I am grieved
For your exit.

You were no coward
You were an entity,
A corps on your own right
You were, sincerely
You were, a carrier

Silent,
You reclined
And watch me repose
My distresses
On your friendly bosom
I'd bubble over
Like the salt for Andrew's liver,
then calm.

Now I look to the sky
Day after day
All I see is patches here and there
I cannot tell your place of respite
Among the Clouds.

Les Faux Amis

You saved your tributes and honour
For when I am no longer here
You saved your healthiest lexicon
For when I am gone.

You put your reserves, the bestest
And the glowing modifiers
Forward, at my interment
On that vigil procession

Because I know it's fashionable
To compose glossy tribute pages
Just so to fulfil funeral decorum
Every indictment is pardoned

I was not unwise, truth be told
To not withhold from me
My own rich textured complements
Of which I know men are unbeatable misers.

The most ornate languages
Are always reserved until the final moments
When a man has lived and died
And his sensations are a doornail.

I was very intentional.
With impressive mix of metaphors
Soothing similes, praise poetry
Elevated eulogies, I baptised me

Was it not hilarious?
That your innuendoes were well matched?
And for your caustic sarcasms?
Did I fail to build bridges with sane syntax?

Never again did I depend
Upon your words of affirmation
Since you ran chronically short of them
I flourished on the positivity of my mine

The thesaurus became my preference
So that when I got weary of an adjective
I replaced it with another
It was a fancy – never a lunacy

In the end, my blight laid bare,
My bleeding halted, I HEALED.
Swifter than I thought.
I convalesced, by my very own encomia.

So, feast or fast at my wake keep
Lay wreaths of orchid
richly fragranced summer fresh
Slash down a cypress bough

Cry yourself oceans from the soul
Give flowery, towering panegyrics
Turn the inside out to claim the medal
For the superlative 'tribute' ever

Ours remain that paradigm of worlds apart
Of a spite at life and plaudits for death
Of a most complex false idea of friendship.

Everything has Ears

I could talk verses with babies in a crib.
You may say they do not listen
That's true.
But I can tell no one is born a listener.
And words, many a time, 5
Do not only look out for listeners,
but hearers too.

Do not crease your face just yet.
Hear me out, I pray you.
If a lullaby sent a baby to slumber 10
That was just a cord of lines
Tied together tenderly,
Yet it works the magic.

I could wander in the woods,
and float in the forests' glades 15
Don't you know the wind performs staves
for the birch, the acacia, and the pine?
And they'll hear. I know they do
Their leaves will sway and boughs will swing
To the tune of an inaudible opera 20

And I often go to the waves
In the still of the night.
With rhymes for recitation
And on those noons of nought

OLUREMI FAYE-ADEMOLA

To offer in exchange for its azure
A hearing of its motion

This is confessional.
I know when the river is hurting
The sea is an ancient deity
With a tempo, a mood and a pace.

Hear fella,
Nothing entirely, goes without ears.

Let the Poet Live

He may speak as one drunken with strong wine
He may act like one suffering paranoia, or weary of soul
Cluttered, he may be incoherent and indiscreet
He may vanish from the voyage
To live in recluse like a hermit
Let the Poet be in his own world.

The world they create for themselves
That space where they often retreat for safety
That entity where they lavish in the luxury of
Words and bask in the plethora of syntagm
That ecosystem where diction is exuberant
That jungle where their concepts are savage
Wild and rude – Let the Poet live in their enclave

That enclave where he carves for himself
That lake from where he takes off
Leave him in that tsunami of ideas
Leave him in that deluge of reflections
Leave him in the fountain of thoughts
Let him wonder liberally in deep meditations
Let him alone to be pensive – do not interject the muse
It's charming when the flow is unstopped

She may have taken flight to Eldorado - a city of reverie
She may be in Greece, miles away, on a solitary isle
She may have been banished by burden
broken and beaten downhill by fatal forces

She may be on a self-imposed exile.
She may be a fugitive of her own imagination
Or even a prisoner of life's intricacies
She may be a victim in the vale of tears
Marooned in the cave of down casting

Or running against the HOUR hand

Leave him, leave her – let the Poet be!

You live, do not forbid the Poet to live.

You Befuddle Me, Truth

'Man is least himself when he talks in his own person.
Give him a mask, and he will tell you the truth.'

(Oscar Wilde)

Why is it so arduous to call a spade a spade?
Why would a man not come real
To his own brethren within his own circle?

Truth, do You mutilate?

Why must a man be in guise to speak You? 5
You are nonetheless the culprit
When the parties involved detach.
When the bottom falls out,
And You emerge from hiding
Like the rediscovery of an espionage 10
This is when the unrest begins,
At Your appearing.
It does not nearly end
You set all against all.
How You feign ignorance 15
Oh the stench of You at the fayre!
That You are never the currency
Strutting arcades of power

OLUREMI FAYE-ADEMOLA

> Why!
> With Your licence to liberate…? 20

> Truth, You befuddle me.

What chances has the gorilla
where the peacock calls for pageantry?
As when the keeper admits:
there is a stunning beauty in the orangutan. 25

The concept of truth completely disconcerts me.

Stitch in the Eardrums

Prologue

Many things which occur by error
Nonetheless, may become fatal.
Whilst many more things will be predestined
A man's journey in life is unprecedented
A clean ride with no dress rehearsals

The phase of the night changes
With some din from jolly juveniles
Stories across the Orient
Of Grecian myths and Arabian folktales
Through the illumination bouncing off the walls
And the moon standing at alert
She remembers it all too clearly
How the middle finger falls out of sync.

A kid having a moment of inquietude
At such time crickets chirp so audibly
One momma in the chamber of a rectory,
Where aunties, uncles, cousins, nieces
Nephews, grand-uncles and aunts
Would often come for respites
Signals her daughter to the bedstead.
It is enough frolicking for the night.

But a filly full of vibrant fiber
Only retires after the last diurnal avian
Then she takes up that unsolicited duty
One of an eternal misadventure
Bloody, open membrane….and gashed palm
Screaming hard like a mutilated prisoner,
In commotion and fury, the mother half-asleep,
Rushes onto the scene.

In the emergency room,
A medico counsels:
Yarn of sinews will stay no longer in synergy,
In spite of the sedulous stitch.

Epilogue

When a mindful mother chides,
That foreboding reverberates.
They bounce back. Only illuminations bounce off…
And a stitch in the ears paves the way
For the misalignment of a lifetime.

What is ... the Night?

The night is deep and dark
    a cocoon for the sun

It is loooooooooong but steady
    to rest the flesh from fatigue

The night is stilled in motion
    faithful harbinger of day

It is lucid ... it is navigable
    for feisty flights of owleries

The night is silent and subtle
    when weaklings flee and warriors duel

It is utter bliss to the composer
    who must fine-tune arrangements of his AUBADE.

    (A parody of Wes Magee's 'What is ... the Sun?')

Dear Ol' Jim

Dear Jim,
How could you say I do not care?
You must have a thing amiss
She drowned you in rum and gin
To soothe your pain at the joint disaster
Of losing Jackie.
Even though she mixed the lethal dose
Resulting in her cardiac arrest
She said Jackie took so much of you – from her.

Dear Jim,
Do you still doubt my affection?
The dentist was going to pluck only two
You were high on sedatives
She was your chaperone
And she urged him to drill out six
Three canines, three incisors
The wisdom ones you went without
A ploy to sabotage the hallowed kiss

Dear Jim,
How could you doubt that I truly care?
It was in full swing winter
When she laundered your overcoat
Saw you off in threadbare jumpers
To your brotherhood at the pub
But she affirmed your foolhardiness

Which you were too slavish to notice
You made a shameless show of you.

Dear Jim,
Never say I hadn't looked out for you
When she came for your charming looks
You wandered away like some insipid sheep
When she gave you your allergies
That beguiling landlady
You ran to my bosom, to my mantelpiece
And there I fostered you. I revived you
You sprang again to life.

Dear Jim,
Dare you say I turned my back on you?
You made your choice when you slid back
To the garden of the enchantress.
You said she loved you in a different way.
Yet you have been a shadow of you ever since.

I heard she made out plans already,
On the grapevine though,
With the funeral directors. Hired pallbearers
To set you high on their shoulders
And bake you dry in their kiln

Dear Jim,
You would scarcely have any headstone.
Your grey will be an earth in her shrubbery
How you were never aware
She supervised your treasures

Frittered away your resources,
Until the pension's weightless
Just like Solomon Grundy
Born for Monday troubles
And by Sunday was no more.

Await your fractured end
The path you chose for you.
What a love in dilemma,
Dear ol' Jim, same ol'.

College Shenanigans

The first time I met my school mother
I don't believe it was a moment of intrigue
I only wanted to meet her
Since that was a portrayal
Of a 'responsible' mademoiselle 5
Then she asked me what was my **Nomenclature**
I nearly fell flat out to the floor.
My feet suddenly became spindly
And could no longer support my build
Mind you, she keenly kept a straight face 10
She wore a pinafore
Over a stripey blue long sleeve shirt
Her wavy kinky hair was held in loose plaits
All the way to the back.
Her stylish spectacles sat upon her nose bridge 15
That caught my fancy to this day.
I was in supplication to wear one too
Once I could convince my poor mother
My eyes were watery
Staring at the chalkboard in class. 20

Soon as the bells chimed,
I ran as fast as my legs would permit.
In the library, like a rat,
I scuttled within the aisles.
I reached for Chambers at first 25
I saw the Websters, too.

Nomenclature (noun) a system for naming things, especially in a particular area of science.
(Cambridge International Dictionary of English)
The librarian would not be drawn into my saga
She just wanted to lock up and leave for the day.

Now the seniors have repaired to the classroom again
For the afterschool prep
But tomorrow is going to be another day
A day and a time to prove
That a junior can retrace their footsteps
In the right direction.
Caught within the grips of restlessness,
That night I tossed to the left and to the right
Tomorrow, I must make right my bloop
I must establish my wits.

The next day at school,
Having neither poise nor balance,
I clambered towards the laboratory
Where my school mother should often be found.

She came up to me at once
Meeting me halfway, she queried
If my *hypothesis* of the last encounter with her
Was sufficient to build an *empirical* ground for connection.

I think I passed out!

Stellar Rush

Spectacularly dusky above,
A body of galaxy pops out
From their hideout, bulgy,
Still on their edges.
I, on the contrary, become flattered
Sitting under a sycamore, I swagger
Into the realm of fantasy.
My heart beats with butter-soft lightness.
I set my soul in cheery mode.
And dollop large wafts of tender currents
If the headhunter advances,
He will abandon his sour mission.
We shall take this flight of fancy together
For his heart also will tinkle like goblets
On the lord of the manor's banqueting,
Waiting to be filled with choice wine.

Upon the lake further afield,
I observe the resplendence
of a thousand constellation
Having the likeness of meteors.
The lake, starkly dark beneath
Tranquil and detached from angsts
Indulges in every romance the sky would offer.

Then I become begrudging
I feel so aggrieved
at the congruence between the elements
My pure adoration
Gradually melts into disdain.

Why do the heavens rape me
Of this cherished nirvana
Well within this tropical viridity?

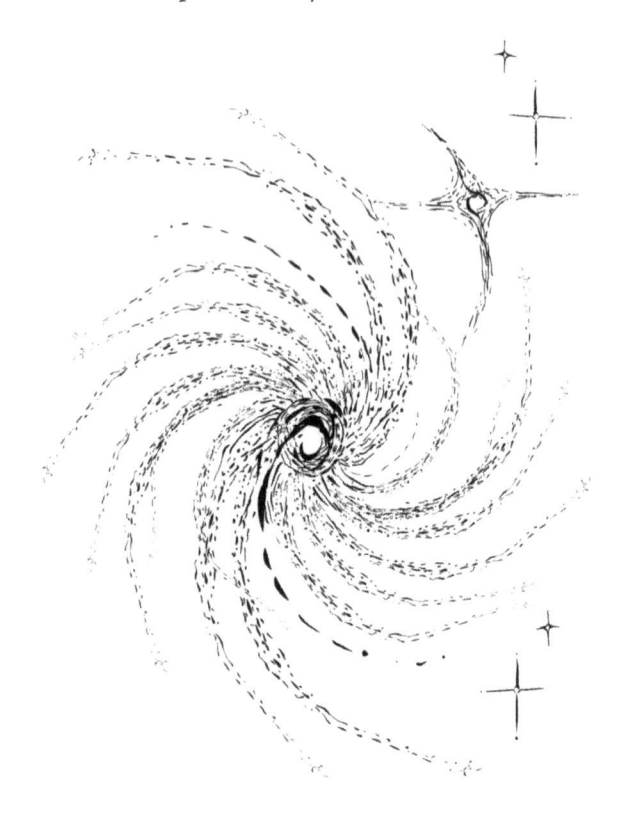

Epitaph

Was it foolishness
To have treasured a thing
Which must someday atrophy …?

But nay, I did not have a choice
Since to treasure without efforts,
Was the least of hair that stuck to your skin.

Elegy

I called to wish you the glad tidings
of a fresh year
on that wintry January night.
I could never have thought
You were only hanging upon a threshold
I could never have believed
How frail and fading!
Because of the eight-hour time zoning
I kept a vigil in London
To perceive your pulse in California

Though it's been well over four years,
I have found no courage still,
to wipe your texts off my phone.
You were the uncle with whom
distance caved in a vast canyon for bonds

this, all the same, does not diminish the ache.
I have always loved how you loved my mother.
And your selfless sacrifices for kinship

It did not matter that fate was hostile
And left a meagre room for fiery ties
It did matter that you showed tolerance
To as many as crossed paths with you
You were that sheath and symbol
Standing in honour of the clan.
And you left palpable prints.

We certainly are left with a crack in the wall
Or best to say, a hollow in our household
But you fill a healthier space - now in Paradise – this, I know.

Goodnight, beloved Uncle David

(Requiescat in pace)

Hardly sated of God's word
A woman of the creed
Who lives on to whet my sword
Herein she falls asleep

Words in any Language

I love words and the beauty of them
I have the greatest affinity for witty words
And like a kid in a candy store
I sometimes stutter on words to exploit
Because am spoilt for choice

I love words and intently study them
Words to dispatch to family, friend or foe alike
And when a fellow's skin lacerates
Or should they bleed in the heart
Words are my potion, a brew
To heal and zip up such wounds

I love words and the sound of them
Jargons, colloquials and street slangs
Words in any language, in any idiolect
And well, when they convey a culture
Giving expression to the literature of life
Words are universal, words are sustainable.

I love words and the shape of them
So what the French would call 'petits pois'
The English calls it 'green peas'
What difference it does make
When one sees *size*, and *colour* the other

You may wonder!
Of all the infinite ocean of words

Some are for right reasons, many for wrong
to make another stick out like a sore thumb.
But life could roll on tastier
Some words, should they never have been dished.

I love words but I do respect the semantics of them
The reason I whittle my diction with sedulity
And if I think I'll go astray with words
I shut my gorge. Hone and hone my lexis
Until they're safe to spill.

Estrangement

That little lamb concealed within
The one that failed to perceive
the glare of the bloated crescent
Or how seasons have changed
The one that swore to itself:
"The turf shall never breed battles.
As a tender scion, terrains would remain."
And convinced at heart how sweet
The ground will not cease to bud
The morning glory and marigold
As day trailed the night.

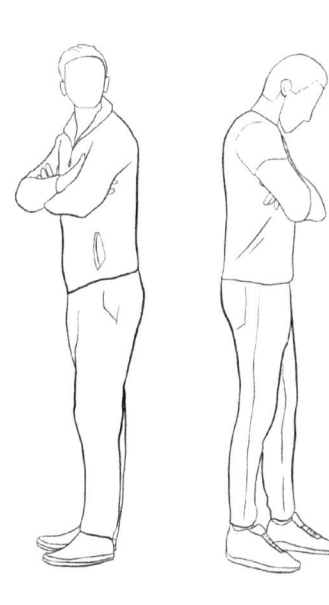

But when the sky alters his fair countenance,
By eventide his light has dimmed
Because the dusk again must set
The veil of blissful ignorance rips apart
That childlike heart much mutilation befalls
Like a dwarf star, faith tapers off
In every direction, are a million shard of glass
So that the vein of the playground
encounters a vicious rupture.
And though blood retains its viscosity,
More frigid than a dead mutton it becomes.

The Right Ones

Who are they?
They were born right
Two heads are a deformity.

They were just born right!

How do they look?
They look like they fell from the Sky?
Oh, yes ... em ... no, they just look right.

Where do they live?
They turned vast forests and dales into empires
And effervescent charters, and that seems right.

When do they become right?
As early as pea pod conceived?
Before the ovum ever swims
in the seminal fluid?
Can't be more right.

For which crafts are they known?
Paean receptors, not certain.
Open to investigation, right?

What do they do?
They do right by the order of edicts and decrees only.
They write the rules, right?

Whose issues are they?
Issues of Feudals, Warlords and Vanquishers

Why are they the right ones?
Violent vendettas. Ruthless conquests
Superiority tussles. Arbitrary settlements.

So then there ought to be the wrong
For there to be the Right, right?

Somehow,
the survival streaks set many a default aright.

RIGHT!!!

Hadassah

What if every man built himself foremost
Before building the world's edifice of grandeur?
Men are a genus, building ships, aeroplanes
Rail tracks and space rockets.
Many men are wizards, the best among the best.

Mordecai, son of Jair, a Benjamite by tribe
Was just a man like every other.
He sat daily at the king's court
He did not build construction gadgets
Like the men who had built the great pyramids of Egypt

He built a damsel.

Upon the time, in Shushan, of a monumental ritual
In dearth of many, this maiden was put out.
And so fair was she, she being herself a captive
Captured the heart of Ahasuerus, The Great!
The king who reigned from India to Ethiopia

The rules were clear; Hegai, the custodian, abiding.
All contenders were to come forward
Unspoiled, undefiled, unblemished
And there, were paraded several virgins
With same bestowal upon each and every maid

This child was who Mordecai had built – Hadassah.
To become the worthy craftmanship of rescue

The one lass to liberate an entire race
This Jew never built branded domestic appliances
Not a thimble did he forge.

Mordecai was not one of those men of masonry
Who built the mighty castle of Ahasuerus
He just sat to observe at the king's gate
With a diligent mind and virtuous antecedents
And putting all of his artistry into enterprise

He built a damsel.

Though this sounds like the cheapest artisanship
Yet, a man's greatest craft is his own ability
To build his character to a scrupulous altitude
And exit leaving rich legacies as trails of his exploits
That, the offspring of Kish achieved by the sternest jury

Mordecai was a man with flesh and blood
A man like every other being, like you, like me
Not different in gene or breed
He was just a man conscientious in his credo
And a fetish for its ordinances, to observe them

This grandson of Shimei, a man with strength of character
Sitting daily at the king's gate seemed a shallow task
He was not one to coordinate the affairs of the palace
Yet he had keen understanding of State business
A man of astuteness

He, it was, who built Hadassah.

Mordecai exuded honour in all facets.
Though he did not build a conglomerate
Nor was a glitzy business empire founded on his charge
He built a crown, a history of ascendant regality
In the most unconventional fashion

Hadassah,
Nurtured by an ordinary man
For another man of might
To preserve ties of kindred
In epic proportions.

An African Child

I am an African child.
Are you, too?
An African child
who sprouts from the African soil
And breathes the African air.
I was nourished with bean cakes at dawn
Fed ladies' fingers at dusk
I ate paprika and scotch bonnet
Kulikuli and Kokoro were my refreshments,
Washed down with Pinto, Kunu and Zobo.

We bathed outdoors,
In the heavy showers of October
Africa, where the sun continually beamed
As we hiked in the verdant lea

Our recreations were hopscotch,
Ayo, Ludo, Snakes & Ladder and Ten-ten
Chess was classy, and for those at the apex
We built sand dunes with mud and clay
Fat worms writhing, cladded in clod
All we silly children, made a blague
When they squirmed at the salt sprinkle

Like the setting of the sun,
Fortunes sometimes descended on us
Then we watched, with great gusto,
The masquerades groove past the alleyways

Legends had it these were wandering spirits
Who once lived in the hoods
Indeed, they were a spectacle and a horror
Best of both for every child,
maybe grown-ups too
They wore quaint garbs with works of haberdashery

To the hearth we returned at sundown
Like humans retreat into mud at sunset
Tales by moonlight
Fables of the old-world crafty tortoise,
How he earned himself a splintered spine
We never stopped short for wisdom
On an African night's entertainment.

I am an African child,
Need I put it one more time on the crescendo?
And of that generation a witness
Of first-hand parents' strivings

Yes, how I love my era
A witness to an enduring parenthood
They did not always get it right
But we learned from them – dignity in labour.

I am an African child.
I absolutely adore my contemporaries,
For we understood eye contacts and body language
Enough to cease from being puerile heads
We dared not talk back at our parents
We did not argue with them,
or a slap with stars reset the brain
Then they charged us to swallow the sob.
The action, the pain. The order, the ache.

Yet those African parents were the real heroes.
Truth be told, they were the celebrities
Back in the day.

I, an African child,
I am that spring that never forgets its source.
I will never feel parched.
I will never trade away my span
For a field of sapphire.
I am an esteemed African child
This conceit shall never ever fade into oblivion.

Glossary

Ayo a boardgame with some carved hollows played with pebble-like seeds.
Kokoro fried cornflour paste eaten as a snack
Kulikuli groundnut cakes eaten as a snack. Its origin is from Northern Nigeria.
Kunu a northern Nigerian brew made from millet with a tendency to undergo fermentation.
Zobo juice extract from dried hibiscus flower or red sorrel drink

Between the Poet and the Songster

Between the prosody of the poet
And the note of the songster,
There are slender strands.
A duo of preachers, both are.
The poet drifted by moods,
And the swing of much muse,
Fleshing out rhymes and rhythms.
The songster traversed oceans
In search of sharps and flats
Bedecking lyrics with wings to fly.

Counsel the poet to be wary
Of the nadir in murky chambers
Lest gloom be churned out to the penchant
This arena oft' needs alliterative clusters
To make supple and merry the heart.

Remind the ready songster
Of alla cappella (casting tunes aside)
Let float the message of the piece
Lest matters of the heart become interred
Beneath the sweetness of accordant melody.

Upon the Midnight Hours

'I was just intending to ask you
for directions to the station,
ma'am' the man said.
'But you seem so scared,' he continued.
'You shouldn't be in the street 5
at this time if you were this petrified.

    The lady stood rooted to one spot,
for she did not at the instance comprehend
   why the man was coming towards her
        in the first place. 10
      She was in the street
     for a different mission,
and she had initially gestured by hand
     to discourage the stranger
from coming too close for comfort. 15

       'Well, just carry on walking
        straight down the road,
       then take the right turn
      by the third traffic lights.
     Walk to the end of that road, 20
and there you are.' replied the lady,
  with apparent fright in her voice.

The man was already striding away,
but managed to mutter a thank you.
Then with some kind of bravery
that seemed to spring from Soweto

'You should not be looking for directions
at 02:30 hours of the night, OK?
you should be in bed.' she retorted.

If you asked me,
from whom could I inquire?
Shouldn't they both be swathed
in the sweet succour of their snug sheets?
It was February – foul and ferocious midwinter
What are the both of them
(the man and the lady)
in the streets for
in the witching hours of the night?
What affairs have kept them both
at these teensy hours, in the streets

Upon deeper reflection,
you may be right to say
both of them are desperate for something.
A thing of high consequences, possibly.
It is certain the trains are not starting out
at this time of the hour,
neither do the night buses
come that way.

Well, I do hope they both find fortune,
These wandering knight and lady in distress, 50
when day breaks and darkness thus vanished.

The throes of a man,
who can ever tell what these are?

The World's too much of a Judge

The world's too much of a judge
They judge you for the things you do
and the things you do not do
The things you say and do not say
They judge your appearance
your dress sense and body frame
whether your fashion is high-end
or you simply espouse a modest style
They judge what you possess and have amassed
in material wealth and what you lack thereupon.
They put you on the echelon
Using a dial, they pin you down
onto the point where they decide
you ought to be according to class, status
stratum or worth that they ascribe to you.
The world will judge your indolence
and judge your diligence alike
They judge you based upon the things
they believe you should attain
They judge you when you fall short
of their own expectations of those attainments
They judge you according to your travel history
Where you have been to and not been
How sumptuous and exotic!
Who you have met, befriended or loved
With whom you have dined and wined
and in whose blithe company you have been
They judge you upon such association

They judge you on the basis of occupation
And the career to which you take a disposition
Your work ethics, how relevant it is
in the open field of mega players
On their own scale of importance,
They judge you for the amount of etiquette
you display and judge you for none of that
They judge you for choosing to be private
and judge you when you are extroverted,
even when you sit in-between (ambivert)
They judge your intelligence and intellect
Your gender and the colour of your skin
    (which you never chose.)
They judge your ethnicity, tribe and tongue
They judge you for your belief systems
Core values, customs, culture and traditions
They judge you for your faith and food preferences,
whether you are teetotal, or an irredeemable boozer
They judge you when you are a lark
You do not escape judgement being an owl either
It is the same world that judges you
for being erudite that will judge your mediocrity.
They will judge you without clemency
Even when they scarcely know you
And have misconceived your person.
The world will judge and judge and judge
Don't you know there's no end to judgement
as long as your lungs inhale oxygen?
The world will judge you
From the sunrise of the cradle
Down to the sunset of the grave.

It is just a world with sparse advocates
And an overabundance of judges
Without the wig and sitting robe,
And neither hoary nor dim-eyed.

Six feet below,
the terminus no one speeds past,
every flesh disintegrates –
the Crucified and Iscariot
all verdicts suddenly cease
all rights of magistracy rescind

Behold the corpse, carrion, carcass, cadaver.
Only termites and maggots doing their own justice
Whilst all the judgements passed as living souls
The Grim Reaper comes as a metaphysical guest
To make an equilibrium of ALL.

Entreaties of the Pragmatist

Oh Heavens,
I ask that you will surround me
with those who reciprocate Respect
Those who are low on Apathy
And those who are high on Tolerance
This will be an elixir from Paradise

I do not ask for any of these:
The perfect chemistry of Naomi and Ruth
The unrivalled bond between David and Jonathan
The allegiance of Pigeons
Or the avowals of Swans
These, in my estimation, will be too much
OLIVERLY, to say the least.
LOVE is severely endangered
LUST is trendier

As the last moonstricken duo were
Romeo and Juliet
Even now I wonder
If they perished remotely for love
Or for mere heroic, classic exploits.

From the modest corner of my heart,
This is not a lofty petition.

Without all of these sincerely settled,
Life is but a walk on eggshells.
So please grant me, oh Heavens.

The Frame

The platitudes of the universe are baffling.
As commonplace as the gilded Sun,
the flickering Moon and glittery Stars.
A thing of absolute wonder that is!

The frame of the deep imagined
without the gregarious forest trees,
the songbirds and calling birds
Without the Oceans and Seas'
violent winds and crashing waves.

Still, it is a great puzzle
What serenades the butterflies
And makes them flip a tango!

Postboxes

Sturdy and bold in streets they stand
A gorging narrow mouth like dell
Many a letter, postcards and notes

Some to say 'I hope you're well'
Some to say 'I miss you so'
Some declare the end to love
A few to sneer to start a fight
Then ones to yield to end a row

Busy, busy all week long
Just to keep the world afloat

Can you spot the red tall vent?
Or some may sit with black beneath
On a lonely winding path

Spring and Autumn all year round
In snow, in rain, in fog and mists
In war, in peace, in loss or finds
Year in, year out through sleet and heat
In streets they stand to glut the mails.

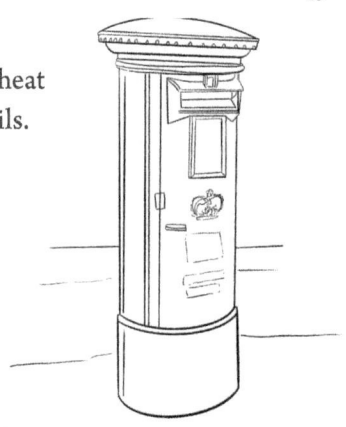

Oluremi Faye-Ademola

Spring Angels

They sprout up en masse
Missionaries on a gospel expedition

Golden yellows, the whites and orange

Testament of bravery
How mortals wriggle out of the frost

The tell-tale child of Spring
Forerunner of the coolest time of year

For when the daffodils are in view
The world foresees the spring is nigh
The landmark of ancient times

They come in fair colours
To rouse the passive minds

They spring on moors, on hills
On fields, by hedgerows
or anywhere really,
dancing like merry maids
Flowers of the West
Proclaiming the opulence
Of springtide.

Daffodils.
Bronzing in the first appearances
Of the sunshine

Then with spring burgeoning,
It's sad to see how they duck

A flight with speedy accents
Just before the bloom.

    (Inspired by William Wordsworth's poem 'I wandered
    lonely as a cloud' otherwise known as 'Daffodils')
    A dedication to all Spring Born

When you said Goodbye

When you said *goodbye*
Your cords were frail and feeble… but beatific
Prodding my wintry pump, I wept.
Bemused by you in genial terms
How you would sound
Ere your roots were inundated.
I saw you in elegance
Festooned with simplicity
I knew you in vigour
Undaunted by the hills
Now in my head, a raging spur – for elegies
Nay in my heart, a gushing pour – for eulogies
For the behoof of you in regal measures.
Mother, you were one of a kind.
Oh, tales by the monstrous moonset
You set sail at dawn
Pick up your chicks with your heart
With feline grace you stride
At dusk, you barely droop
In spite of the bleak, blank view
Unflinching in your demeanour
Then I in wonder ponder:
What potter immortal framed you?
What steward strong, resolute you are!
Renaissance woman.
My first true mistress of grand integrity
Some four decades you lavished on your nation
That she might be unwavering in foundation

Tilling, toiling, travailing.
You surpassed the scars
Giving life, living life
My heroine, meticulous model of diligence
Agilely composed till octogenarian
Only then did you toddle
You went from a flint
And trudged like a groggy sapling
I cannot say *'goodbye'*
Rather, I will bid *'au revoir'*
May that not be same as a dingy farewell
'Maman, by the pearly gates,
Past the chasm ... we shall, someday, reunite.

Distractions at the Square

At dawn, she rises up,
takes down her hanging basket
reties her wrapper around her waist
then she makes a loose padded knot
And sets out for the early bargains.

A stretchy, lonely walk to the square
Past the quarry, past the old mill
The foundry and village headmaster's yard
On a brick-burnt, dusty narrow road
And oh, past the little corner parish.

A market day, a bustling hushy-pushy day
When the haggling chimes on end
like the bell on the tower of the square
Where the makeshifts are rowdy rough
like the urban squatter camps.

First port of call, the bakery
Smell of scones, cakes and hot cross buns
wafting towards the southern axis
The parlour with a two mice chase
But the baker has a cat
dealing with the mess of mice!

Then she stops at the greens stall
Every produce seemingly spotless
You would think she must be impressed

By the robust rude-healthy garden eggs
That sit in boxes made of dry straw

Next, she advances the veal and mutton
Fresh from the butchery, still dripping red
Slaughterhouses are a gambling ground
While the cocks squawk about the coop.
She's keen on settling for 'cured'

This time, it's at the herbs and pulses
Sage, chives, parsley, oregano and fennel
How they spice up the grocer's stand
The pulses, glossy skinned, with creamy flesh
Yet she returns no verdict.

Fishmongers having idle jaws and banters
Ten one quarter pound of the eve's escapades
Like a man's blistering catch of a maiden
She chuckles. Feels the haddock, plaice and cod
But still, makes no move.

It's twilight.
Absurdity of all insanity!

The sky makes ready to empty its bowels
There's a let lose unannounced.
like an intoxicated sot in a fit of rage.
But an empty basket will shield none
just like it will hold no rainwater down.

Please do not enquire from me
how she makes her way back home.
I hope by heavens, you know already
How some people set out so early
Yet their pilgrimage and purpose
is never as clearly defined.

50

Written in August

Two scores precisely
On a scorching Sunday
You bade us bye

Your daughter with pastel red flannel
And I, with the vessel in place

Your digits were curved in
For they were now flaccid
You had wasted colour in the skin
While your lips were warped

I remembered,
When you first taught me
How to crackle my knuckles

Like a militant in combat,
Your breath wrestled.
You slurred at first
Before you lost your speech,
So then you gestured
Only with the corner of your eyeballs.
Your body laid on the four-poster
Wilting and pale-faced
Like the sliver of a waning moon

We became wholly enervated
Many times, solemn and distant.

There were no expressive phrases
To connect the worst of our fears
Silence engulfed the foyer
Like an inferno.

My niece and I,
We lost the courage of eye contact
A moment laden with improper burden

Umpteenth time for two hearts
Together skipping beats
Whereupon, the fluids within froze.

Suddenly, as if with intrepid scorn
You hawked up a snort
One which has been smouldering for weeks

I thought that was you
The snotty you
Ridding a cloud of dust
As you would, doing chores at home.

But hell no!

That was your final breath
A self-assertion
You flung in the face
of the monster calling.

(In cherished memory of Monisola)

Eyes of Innocence

'Christ is the head of this house
The unseen guest at every meal
The silent listener to every conversation.'

On every wall, in every residence
In the 197something...
Such was the framed phrase.

I made sure to finish my supper
At every mealtime by the scraps,
An abhorrence is the sight of a ghost
Feasting on food remnants.
I whispered every discourse
Since I hated a scheming eavesdropper
Not to hear much good of himself.

As for the head of the house,
An impalpable one, in my puny mind,
Meant gaining extra playtime,
And sneaking down into the pantry
To gobble up more caramel and
coconut candy.

Psalm 419

Once I watched the chimpanzee
Hunt down the colobus monkey
In a merciless monstrous barricade
Across the feral jungle.

My blood boiled over,
That a predator would choose
Its own kith and kin, its own bloodline
One of likeness and semblance, as prey.

Suddenly, a nettlesome prod from within
Ambushed me as on to Golgotha I reeled
A culpable despicable chimp
To atone for this atrocious act

So then I refrained from judgement
These brutal breaths of beasts…
Are only a replica
Of human malevolence

My arms fell out of hollows
Disjointed from the scapula.
Filled still with indignation,
I burst open and spouted my spleen.

Milton Keynes UK
Ingram Content Group UK Ltd.
UKHW022309050424
440645UK00005B/267